LIFE CYCLES
Robins

by Robin Nelson

first step nonfiction

Lerner Publications Company · Minneapolis

Look at the robin.

Robins sing in the trees.

A robin is a **bird**, like a duck or an owl.

How does a robin grow?

A robin starts as a blue egg.

The eggs are in a **nest**.

A mother robin keeps the
eggs warm.

One day, the eggs **hatch**.

Baby robins are called **chicks**.

The chicks cannot fly.

The mother and father
robins bring the chicks food.

They eat insects, worms, and **berries**.

The chicks grow feathers
and get bigger.

They learn to fly and find
food.

This robin is grown up.

It is fun to watch a robin grow.

beak

eye

wing

tail
feathers

legs

Adult Robins

Adult robins have red orange feathers on their breasts. Males have darker feathers on their heads and tails than females.

When the weather turns cold, robins fly south, or migrate, to warmer climates. In the spring, the robins come back and begin a new life cycle.

Robin Facts

 A mother robin lays two to four eggs at a time.

 It takes 12 to 16 days for robin eggs to hatch.

 A robin's egg is about the size of a quarter.

 Baby robins are called chicks until they are strong enough to leave the nest. Then they are called fledglings.

When chicks first hatch, they cannot open their eyes. They will open them in about five days.

 Robins talk to one another by singing.

 Robins build their nests out of dead grass, twigs, and mud.

 The robin is the state bird of Connecticut, Michigan, and Wisconsin.

Glossary

 berries – small, juicy fruit

 bird – an animal that lays eggs and has wings and feathers

 chicks – baby robins

 hatch – come out of an egg

nest – a basket made of mud and grass that birds build to hold their eggs

Index

The images in this book are used with the permission of: U.S. Fish and Wildlife Service, pp. 2, 16, 22 (top); © Jim Zipp/Photo Researchers, Inc., p. 3; © iStockphoto.com/Paul Tessier, p. 4; © Marvin Dembinsky Photo Associates/Alamy, pp. 5, 22 (second from top); © Dwight Kuhn, pp. 6, 7, 12, 13, 14, 22 (center); © Richard Day/Animals Animals, pp. 8, 22 (bottom); © Alan & Sandy Carey/Peter Arnold, Inc., pp. 9, 22 (second from bottom); © Richard T. Nowitz/ National Geographic/Getty Images, p. 10; © John Cornell/Visuals Unlimited, p. 11; © Don Enger/Animals Animals, p. 15; © Arthur Morris/Visuals Unlimited, p. 17; © Laura Westlund/ Independent Picture Service, p. 18, 20, 21.
Front Cover: © Michael Woodruff/Dreamstime.com.

Lerner Publications Company
A division of Lerner Publishing Group, Inc.
241 First Avenue North
Minneapolis, MN 55401 U.S.A.

Website address: www.lernerbooks.com

Library of Congress Cataloging-in-Publication Data

Nelson, Robin, 1971–
    Robins / by Robin Nelson.
       p.   cm. — (First step nonfiction. Animal life cycles)
    Includes index.
    ISBN: 978–0–7613–4068–3 (lib. bdg. : alk. paper)
    1. Robins—Life cycles—Juvenile literature.
    I. Title.
    QL696.P288N45 2009
    598.8'42—dc22   2008029621

Manufactured in the United States of America
1 2 3 4 5 6 – DP – 14 13 12 11 10 09